HOW OUR MUSCLES WORK

Text: Victoria Ávila
Illustrations: Antonio Muñoz Tenllado

El músculo, órgano de la fuerza © Copyright Parramón
Ediciones, S.A. Published by Parramón Ediciones, S.A.,
Barcelona, Spain.

How Our Muscles Work copyright © 1995 by Chelsea House
Publishers, a division of Main Line Book Co.

3 5 7 9 8 6 4 2

Músculo, órgano de la fuerza. English.
   How our muscles work.
      p. cm. — (Invisible world)
   Includes index.
   ISBN 0-7910-3150-0
   1. Muscles—Physiology—Juvenile literature.
[1. Muscular system.] I. Chelsea House Publishers. II. Title.
III. Series.
QP321. M89813 1995   94-28304
612.7'4—dc20   CIP
                                                        AC

Contents

INVISIBLE WORLD

HOW OUR MUSCLES WORK

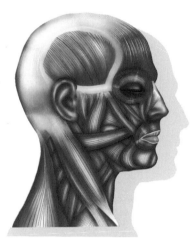

CHELSEA HOUSE PUBLISHERS

Philadelphia

The Functions of Muscles

Muscles enable us to run, jump, dance, laugh, swallow, breathe, smile—a whole range of movements. The locomotive apparatus, composed of bones, joints, and muscles, makes it possible for us to move. Skeletal muscles are the fibrous tissues that cover the bones. Joints are the structures that link the bones together.

There are over 400 muscles in the body. Skeletal muscles are the most numerous type; they account for nearly half of a person's total body weight. Other muscles perform functions unrelated to the locomotive apparatus, providing involuntary movements that keep bodily organs and systems running smoothly.

Muscles do much more than simply move our limbs and let us flex like bodybuilders. One type of muscle, which joins the skin to bone, allows us facial expression. The muscles of the thorax and the abdomen make breathing possible, while the muscles of the esophagus, the stomach, and the intestines contract and relax so that our bodies can digest food. In fact, the whole body is powered by the cardiac muscle or myocardium in the heart.

A view of the outer skeletal muscle structure, the key to voluntary movement. ▶

The muscles which form the internal walls of the esophagus push a bolus of food from the pharynx to the stomach. These peristaltic contractions are so powerful that they can even act against gravity, allowing us to swallow upside down. ▶

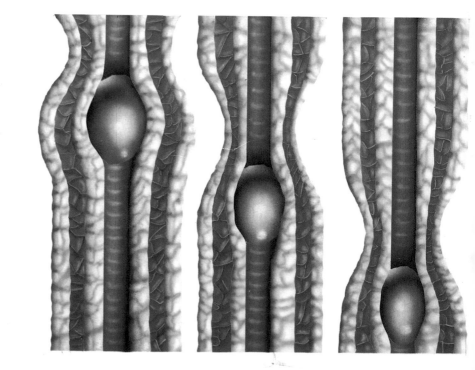

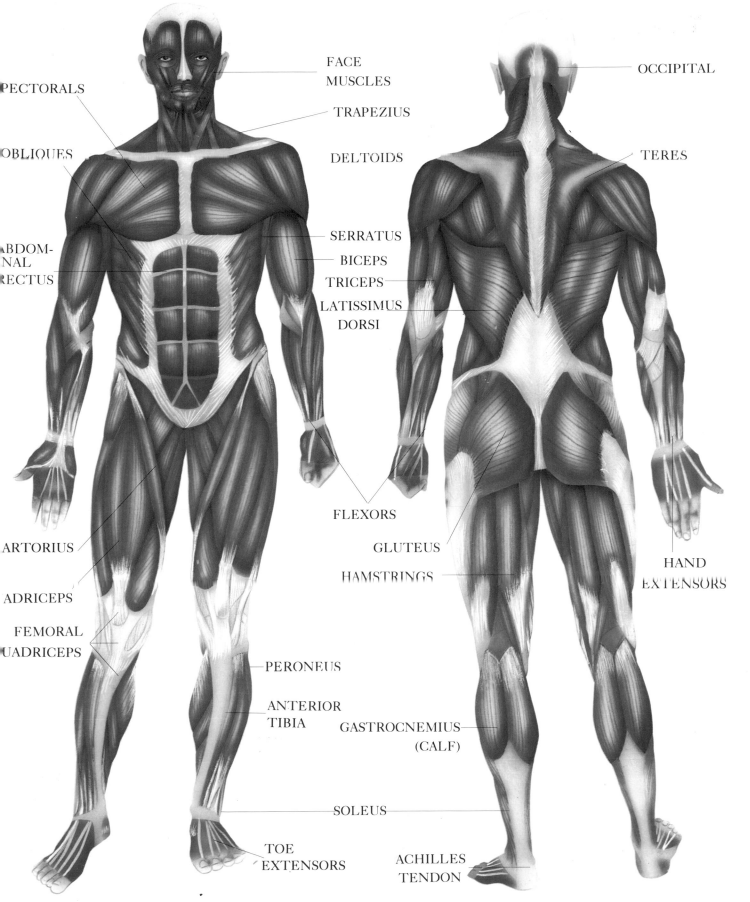

PECTORALS

OBLIQUES

ABDOM-
NAL
RECTUS

ARTORIUS

ADRICEPS

FEMORAL
QUADRICEPS

FACE
MUSCLES

TRAPEZIUS

DELTOIDS

SERRATUS

BICEPS

TRICEPS

LATISSIMUS
DORSI

FLEXORS

GLUTEUS

HAMSTRINGS

PERONEUS

ANTERIOR
TIBIA

GASTROCNEMIUS
(CALF)

SOLEUS

TOE
EXTENSORS

ACHILLES
TENDON

OCCIPITAL

TERES

HAND
EXTENSORS

What Are They Made Of?

The body has three types of muscles: skeletal, smooth, and cardiac. Skeletal muscles, which are connected to bones by tendons, consist of long, cylindrically shaped cells called fibers. These striated fibers possess several nuclei and have light and dark bands formed by the protein myofilaments actin and myosin. Each muscle fiber is wrapped in a thin membrane named the sarcolemma, grouped into bundles called fascicles, and then connected by perimysium tissue.

Smooth muscle, which controls automatic or involuntary movements, is not linked to bones. While its fibers also possess myofibrils made of actin and myosin, the proteins are not arranged in light and dark bands. These fibers are shorter than skeletal muscle cells and contain only one nucleus.

Cardiac muscle cells, strung together into striated fibers, usually have only one nucleus and many mitochondria, which produce energy for the cell.

Although it resembles skeletal fiber, the myocardium is involuntary.

Muscle can also be classified according to its shape. Sphincter muscles, which control openings in the body such as the mouth, are circular. Some muscles are fan-shaped or wide and flat, while many skeletal muscles are long and tapered.

Notice the fiber differences in the three kinds of muscles. ▶

CIRCULAR

Circular muscles open and close different orifices and tubes in the body. Short muscles are small, with precise functions, while flat muscles play a role in the whole breathing process. Long or fusiform muscles, such as the biceps in the arms, affect locomotion. ▶

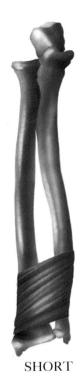

SHORT

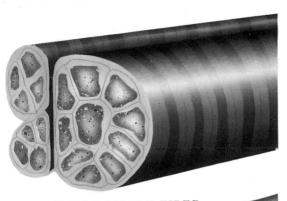

SKELETAL MUSCLE FIBER

MYOCARDIUM

SMOOTH MUSCLE FIBER

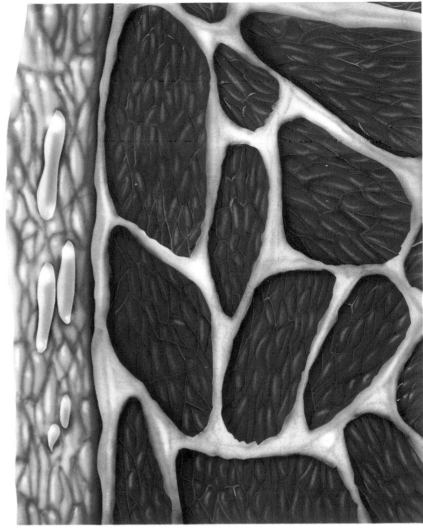

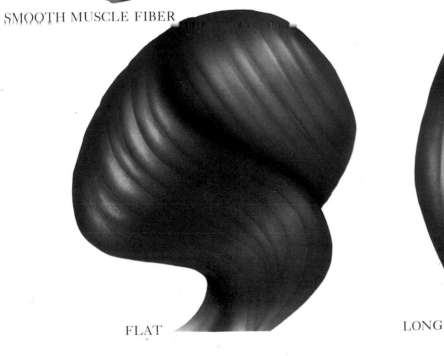

FLAT

LONG

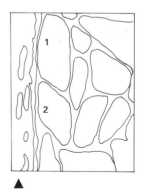

▲

In this cross-section, it is possible to distinguish the muscle fibers (1) and the bundles which they form (2).

Voluntary and Involuntary

During a jump, an array of voluntary muscles in this man's limbs are contracting to produce the range of movement shown. At the same time, involuntary muscles are making it possible for him to breathe air and circulate blood.

▼

Voluntary muscles are the type we can move whenever we want. They are made of grooved fibers, and apart from a few small muscles such as the orbicular oculi of the eyes, they all form part of the locomotive apparatus.

The brain sends its commands along motor neurons, which connect to individual muscle fibers. These nerves release chemicals called neurotransmitters that stimulate the myofibrils of actin and myosin to link together, causing a muscle contraction. During a contraction, the length of the muscle is reduced and enough force is generated to bend an arm or leg.

Involuntary muscles, which are not under our control, perform automatic actions that are vital for the correct functioning of the body. Almost always made of smooth fiber, involuntary muscles play a critical part in processes as varied as respiration, circulation, and digestion.

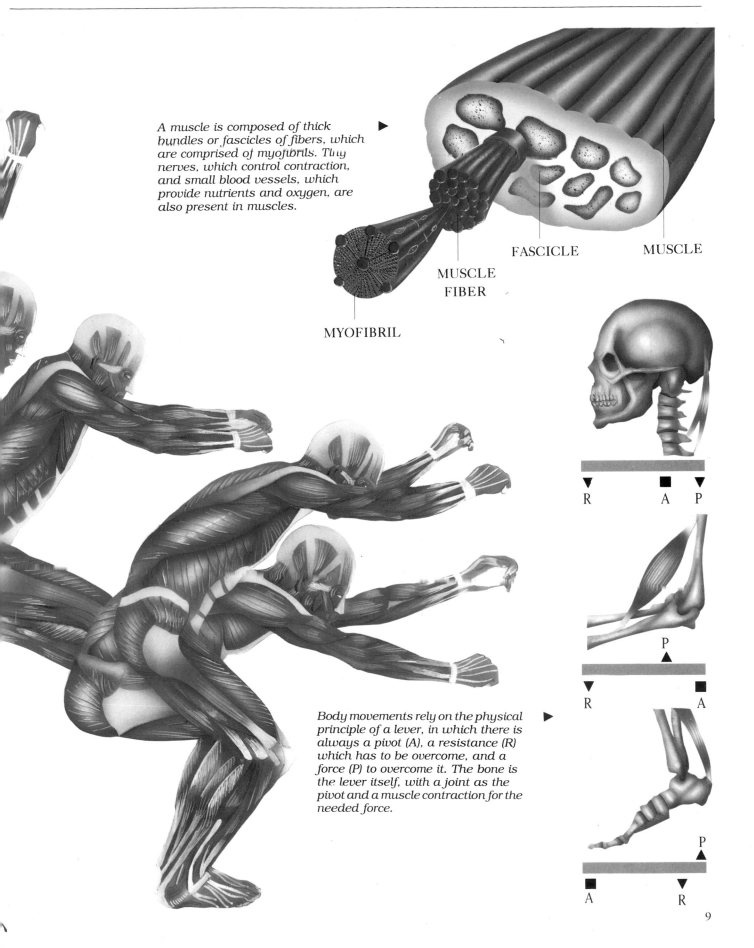

A muscle is composed of thick bundles or fascicles of fibers, which are comprised of myofibrils. Tiny nerves, which control contraction, and small blood vessels, which provide nutrients and oxygen, are also present in muscles. ▶

FASCICLE

MUSCLE

MUSCLE FIBER

MYOFIBRIL

R   A   P

P

R   A

Body movements rely on the physical principle of a lever, in which there is always a pivot (A), a resistance (R) which has to be overcome, and a force (P) to overcome it. The bone is the lever itself, with a joint as the pivot and a muscle contraction for the needed force. ▶

P

A   R

9

An Energetic Machine

Physical exercise benefits the whole body because regular muscular activity strengthens the heart, increases the lungs' capacity, and boosts the production of energy. During strenuous activity, you become hot and sweaty because muscular activity generates calorific energy.

In order to contract, the muscle needs energy from a chemical compound called ATP, which is manufactured in the cells by mitochondria. When its small ATP supply is consumed, the muscle must rely on cellular respiration to metabolize more from glucose, a food sugar that is stored in the muscles as glycogen. In aerobic respiration, oxygen from the bloodstream helps the muscle cell to break down glucose into carbon dioxide and water, releasing a great deal of energy in the process.

If the muscles do not receive enough oxygen, the cells must turn to anaerobic respiration, which transforms the glucose into lactic acid and produces much less energy. When lactic acid accumulates, it causes stiffness, a muscle pain you may have experienced after an intense workout.

Aerobic respiration or metabolism uses oxygen to transform glucose into carbon dioxide and water, releasing energy in the form of ATP. If the body is not in shape for intense physical exercise, not enough oxygen reaches the muscles and anaerobic metabolism takes place. A by-product of this respiration is lactic acid, which builds up and makes muscle contractions more difficult.

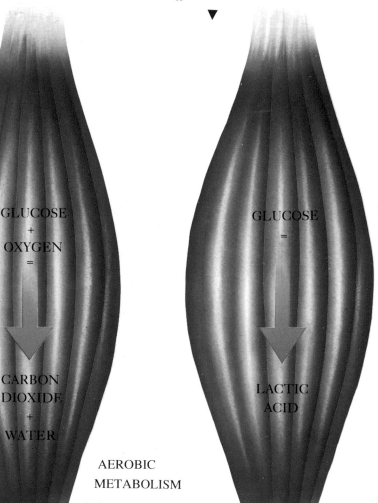

ANAEROBIC
METABOLISM

GLUCOSE
+
OXYGEN
=

CARBON
DIOXIDE
+
WATER

AEROBIC
METABOLISM

GLUCOSE
=

LACTIC
ACID

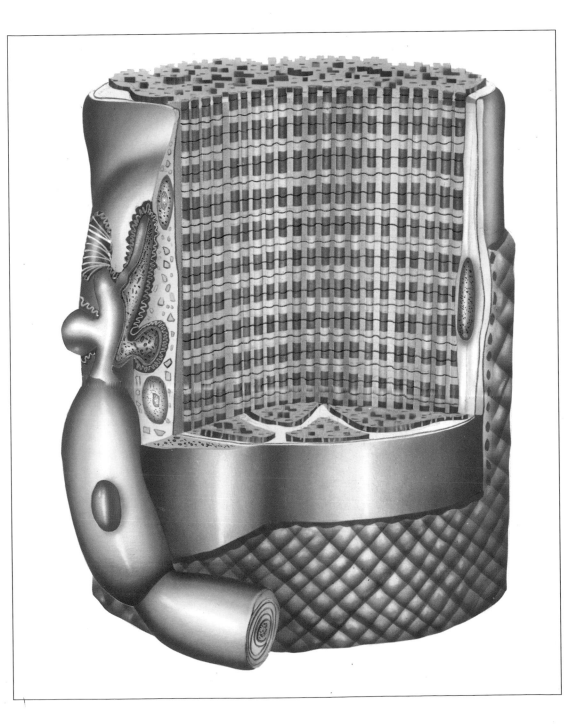

Muscles consist of myofibrils (1), which determine the longitudinal grooves of the muscle fiber. The presence of other transversal striations called sarcomeres (2) characterizes the voluntary muscles of the locomotive apparatus.

▼

Locomotive Apparatus: Muscles, Joints, and Bones

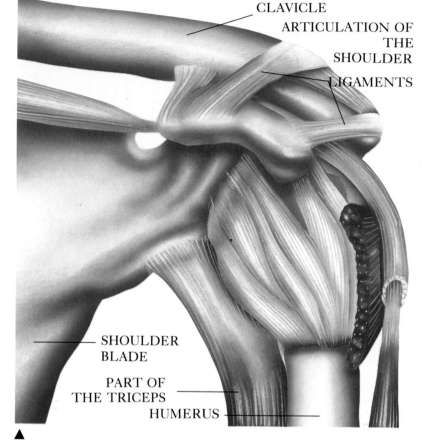

CLAVICLE

ARTICULATION OF THE SHOULDER

LIGAMENTS

SHOULDER BLADE

PART OF THE TRICEPS

HUMERUS

The locomotive apparatus of bones, joints, and skeletal muscles makes movement possible. The bone acts as a lever, pivoting against the joint with force from the muscle. The extent of these motions depends on the shape and arrangement of the bones and joints.

Synovial joints, the only kind which provide free movement, are found in the shoulder, the elbow, the knee, the hip, the wrist, the ankle, and the foot. Different kinds of synovial joints include the gliding joint in the wrist, which allows bones to move side to side and back and forth, and the hinge joint in the elbow, which permits movement in only one up-and-down direction.

Just as the muscles carry out a protective role for certain bodily organs, the joints offer some protection to the bones. Cartilage cushions the bones from shock, and synovial fluid lubricates the area to ease friction.

▲ *The ball-and-socket joint in the shoulder makes a wide range of motion possible: forward elevation, lateral elevation, and rotation.*

The knee joint contains two hard cartilages, the menisci, which increase the area of contact between the femur and the tibia. The knee has lateral, ventral, and dorsal ligaments as well as cruciate or crossed ligaments inside to aid stability. ▶

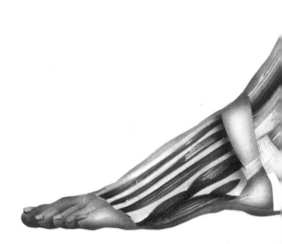

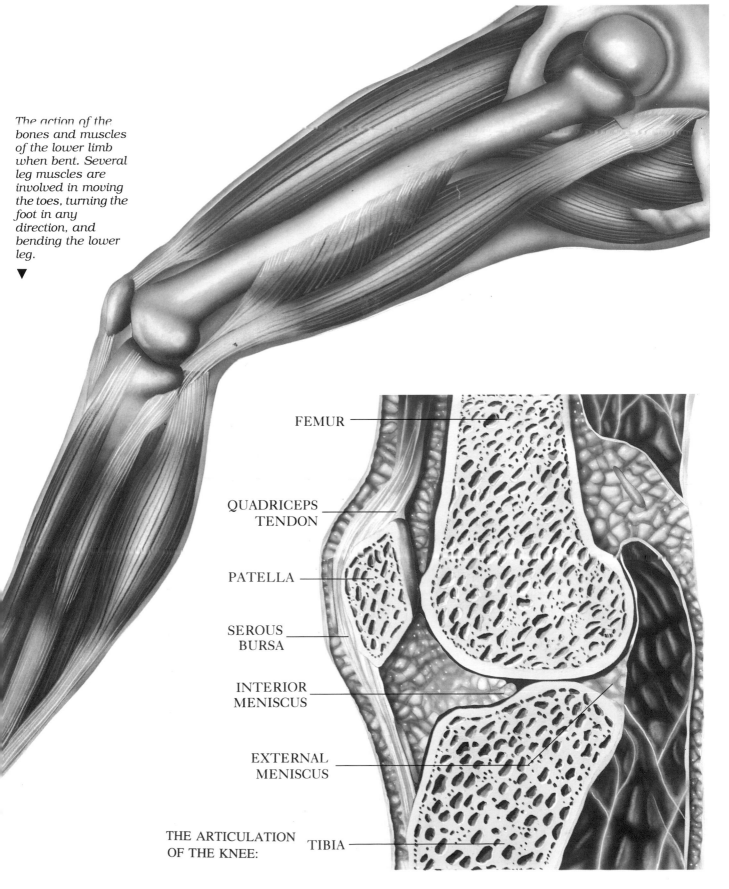

The action of the bones and muscles of the lower limb when bent. Several leg muscles are involved in moving the toes, turning the foot in any direction, and bending the lower leg.

▼

FEMUR

QUADRICEPS TENDON

PATELLA

SEROUS BURSA

INTERIOR MENISCUS

EXTERNAL MENISCUS

THE ARTICULATION OF THE KNEE:

TIBIA

Arms and Legs, Bursting with Movement

The muscles of the upper limbs can be divided into four parts. The shoulder's deltoids raise and lower the arm. The arm's most important muscles, the biceps in the front and the triceps at the back, are antagonistic muscles, which means they perform opposing actions to flex or extend the forearm. The forearm has supinators and pronators, which allow the turning motion of the forearm, the rotation of the hands, and the flexing and extending of the fingers. The hand's small, short muscles are purely for moving the fingers.

The muscles of the lower limbs are also grouped into four different areas. The three gluteal muscles in the pelvis which form the buttocks hold the torso upright, permitting humans to walk on two legs. Thigh muscles such as the quadriceps aid in motion, while the muscles of the lower leg, attached to the heel by the Achilles tendon, flex and extend the foot. Finally, the foot contains small muscles which move the toes and make walking easier.

The two types of fibers within these skeletal muscles can affect athletic performance. Slow-twitch fibers contract more slowly, take longer to break down ATP, and rely more on aerobic respiration than fast-twitch fibers do. People with a majority of fast-twitch fibers in their legs are more likely to be better sprinters, while people with more slow-twitch fibers may achieve their best in long-distance races.

MUSCLES
OF THE
UPPER LIMBS

REAR VIEW   FRONT VIEW

DELTOIDS

INFRASPINATUS

TRICEPS

BICEPS

VASTUS
EXTERIOR

HAND
EXTENSORS

HAND
EXTENSORS

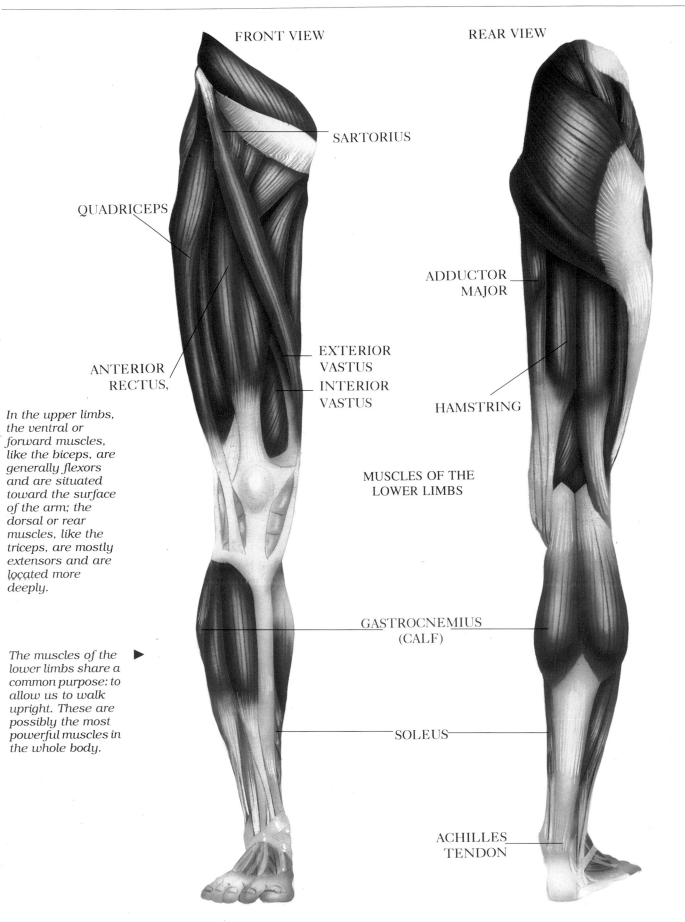

FRONT VIEW

REAR VIEW

SARTORIUS

QUADRICEPS

ADDUCTOR
MAJOR

ANTERIOR
RECTUS,

EXTERIOR
VASTUS

INTERIOR
VASTUS

HAMSTRING

*In the upper limbs,
the ventral or
forward muscles,
like the biceps, are
generally flexors
and are situated
toward the surface
of the arm; the
dorsal or rear
muscles, like the
triceps, are mostly
extensors and are
located more
deeply.*

MUSCLES OF THE
LOWER LIMBS

*The muscles of the
lower limbs share a
common purpose: to
allow us to walk
upright. These are
possibly the most
powerful muscles in
the whole body.*

GASTROCNEMIUS
(CALF)

SOLEUS

ACHILLES
TENDON

15

Which Muscles Do We Use To Smile and To Chew?

There are numerous small, voluntary muscles in the face and head area which perform two main functions. The masticators ensure the movement of the lower jawbone, enabling us to chew food. The versatile facial muscles, joined to the skin and the bone, allow us to communicate without words by smiling, winking, frowning, and making other meaningful expressions.

The thick, resistant muscles of the neck fulfill a very important role by covering the bones which connect the head to the torso and allowing a full range of head movement. On each side of the neck lies a very powerful muscle, the sternomastoid, which allows the rotating and bending movements of the head. The trapezius, which covers the neck, is a muscle from the thorax which extends to the back of the neck and links the head to some vertebrae and ribs.

A view of the many muscles in the face and neck. The orbicular oculi and the orbicular orbis, both sphincter muscles, control the opening and closing of the eyelid and the mouth, respectively. ▶

OCCIPITAL

TEMPORALIS

MASSETER

POSTERIOR
AURICULAR

BUCCINATOR

PTERYGOID

MUSCLES
OF THE
HEAD AND NECK

SERRATUS

TRAPEZIUS

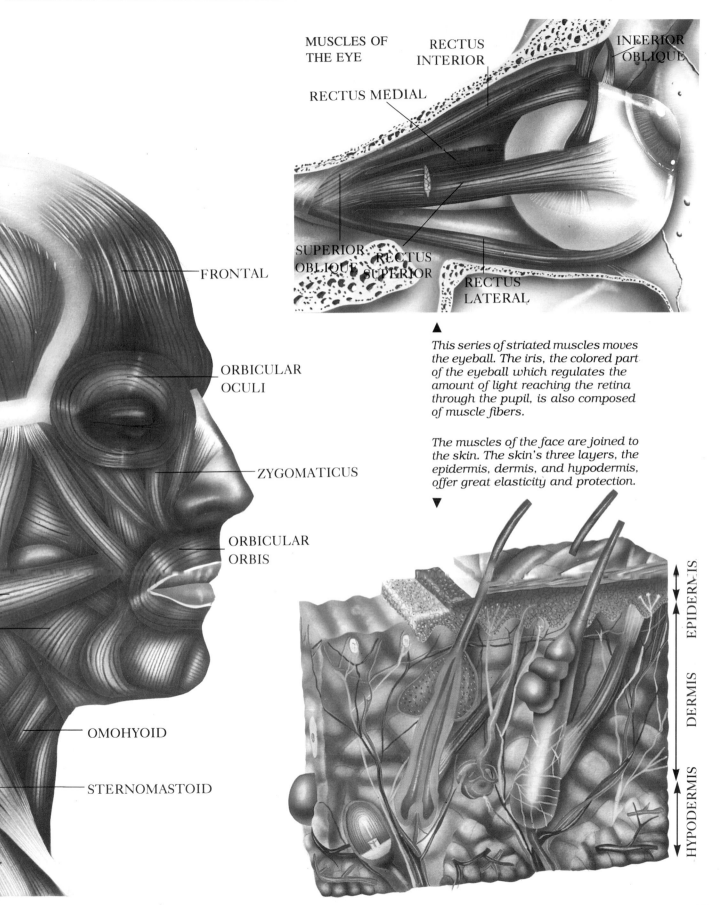

MUSCLES OF
THE EYE

RECTUS
INTERIOR

INEERIOR
OBLIQUE

RECTUS MEDIAL

SUPERIOR
OBLIQUE

RECTUS
SUPERIOR

RECTUS
LATERAL

This series of striated muscles moves the eyeball. The iris, the colored part of the eyeball which regulates the amount of light reaching the retina through the pupil, is also composed of muscle fibers.

The muscles of the face are joined to the skin. The skin's three layers, the epidermis, dermis, and hypodermis, offer great elasticity and protection.

FRONTAL

ORBICULAR
OCULI

ZYGOMATICUS

ORBICULAR
ORBIS

OMOHYOID

STERNOMASTOID

EPIDERMIS

DERMIS

HYPODERMIS

The Diaphragm, A Crucial Muscle

The respiratory system takes in air to acquire the oxygen necessary for proper cell functioning and eliminates carbon dioxide, the by-product of internal respiration. The torso, which stretches from the shoulders to the pelvis, has two parts, the thorax and the abdomen, both of which house muscles key to breathing.

The thorax, situated above the waist, contains the heart and the lungs and is protected by the part of the skeleton called the thoracic cage. The main muscles of the thorax are the pectorals, which raise the arms when contracted, and the serratus muscles, which lift the ribs when we exhale.

Between the thoracic cavity and the abdominal cavity lies the most important muscle in the respiratory system: the diaphragm, which is underneath the lungs. When relaxed, the diaphragm is in its most arched position, exerting pressure on the ribs and reducing the volume of the thorax. When it contracts, it lessens its umbrella shape, allowing the lungs enough space to inhale.

Located in the abdomen, the obliques perform the opposite task to the diaphragm when they contract, pulling the ribs down and expelling air from the lungs. The contractions of the rectus, which covers the stomach area, allow the waist to bend and also play a role in the respiratory process.

The abdominal cavity is completely covered by muscles which protect its contents, facilitate breathing, and aid torso movement.

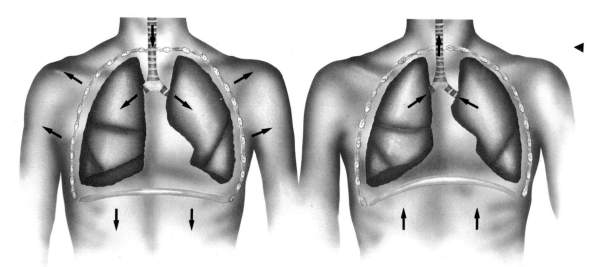

Lying underneath the lungs in the thoracic cavity, the diaphragm plays a crucial role in the respiration process, falling during inhalation and rising during exhalation.

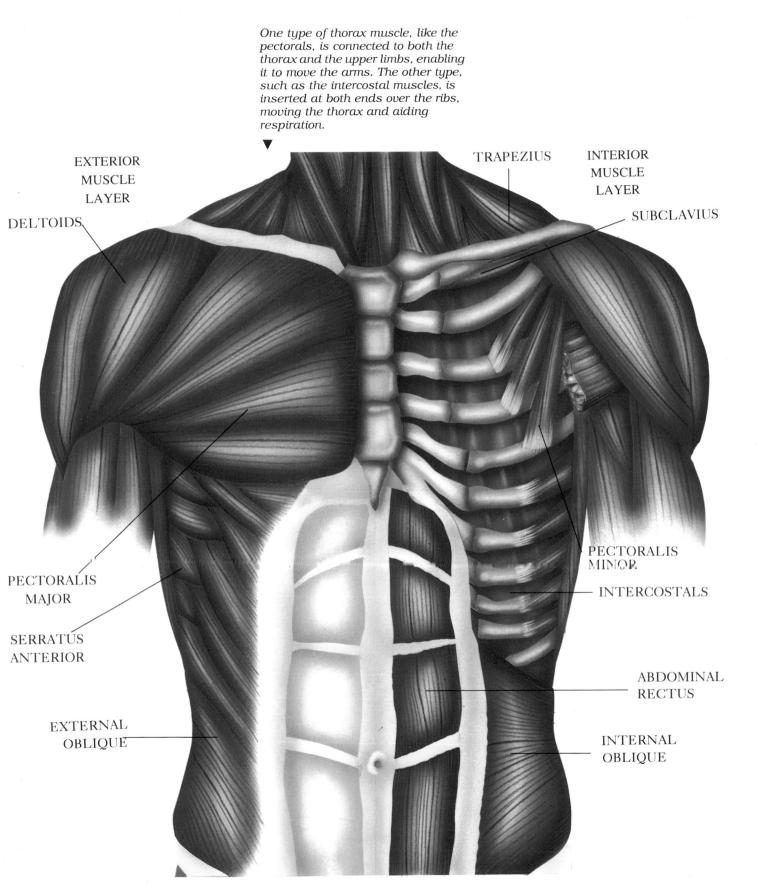

One type of thorax muscle, like the pectorals, is connected to both the thorax and the upper limbs, enabling it to move the arms. The other type, such as the intercostal muscles, is inserted at both ends over the ribs, moving the thorax and aiding respiration.

EXTERIOR MUSCLE LAYER

TRAPEZIUS

INTERIOR MUSCLE LAYER

DELTOIDS

SUBCLAVIUS

PECTORALIS MINOR

INTERCOSTALS

PECTORALIS MAJOR

SERRATUS ANTERIOR

ABDOMINAL RECTUS

EXTERNAL OBLIQUE

INTERNAL OBLIQUE

A System for Digestion

The digestive system, which stretches nearly 40 feet from the mouth to the anus, includes the esophagus, the stomach, the small intestine, the large intestine, and the muscles which line these organs. A series of physical, chemical, and biological changes occurs in this system, breaking food down into nutrients in two stages. In the mechanical stage, the tongue—the most muscular organ in the body—pushes food between the teeth, and the masticators move the teeth in a chewing action. This chewing, combined with saliva, forms a bolus of food that is easily swallowed.

The contractions of the esophagus's muscles push the bolus down into the stomach, where the chemical stage of digestion begins in full force. While the stomach's muscles continue to mix the food through peristaltic movements, gastric juices transform proteins into amino acids.

Next the food passes through the pylorus, the sphincter muscle which opens and closes one end of the stomach, into the small intestine. More than 20 feet long, the small intestine is divided into three sections: the duodenum, the jejunum, and the ileum. By the time the food reaches the ileum, secretions from the liver and the pancreas have completely processed the food into nutrients which can be absorbed by the many tiny blood vessels in the small intestine. The waste matter that could be neither digested nor absorbed constitutes the feces, which travels through the cecum, the colon, and the rectum in the large intestine. At each of these stages, muscles keep the process moving smoothly.

As it travels through the digestive tract, food undergoes a series of physical, chemical, and biological changes. After it is mechanically broken down in the mouth, the muscles in the digestive system propel the food through the esophagus, the stomach, and the small and large intestines. By the end of this process, vital nutrients have been absorbed into the bloodstream and waste matter expelled.

DIGESTIVE SYSTEM

MOUTH

PHARYNX

ESOPHAGUS

LIVER

STOMACH

PANCREAS

SMALL AND LARGE INTESTINE

RECTUM

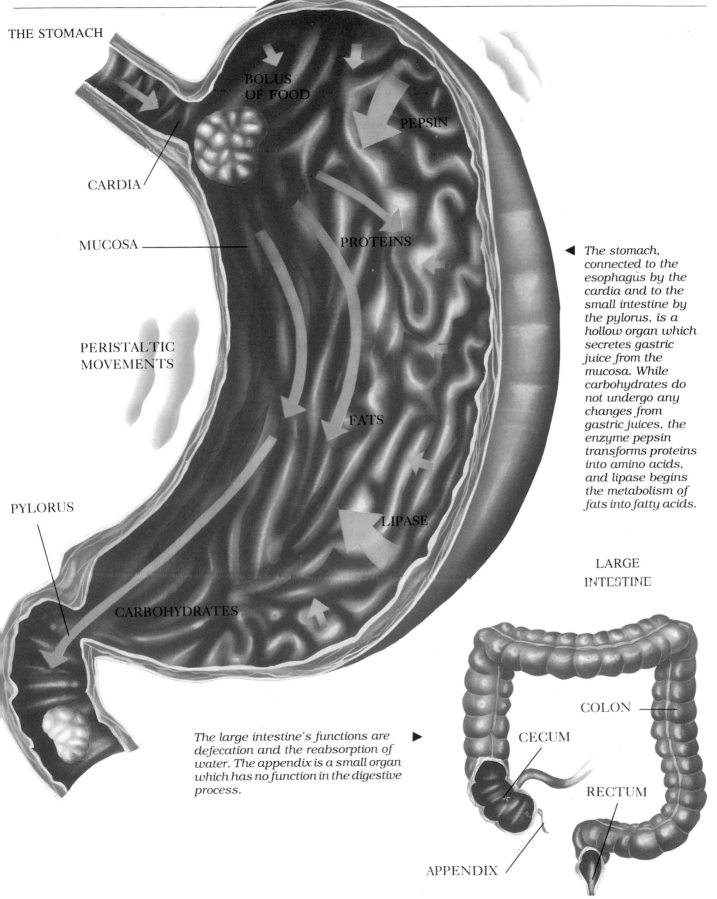

THE STOMACH

BOLUS OF FOOD

PEPSIN

CARDIA

MUCOSA

PROTEINS

PERISTALTIC MOVEMENTS

FATS

PYLORUS

LIPASE

CARBOHYDRATES

The stomach, connected to the esophagus by the cardia and to the small intestine by the pylorus, is a hollow organ which secretes gastric juice from the mucosa. While carbohydrates do not undergo any changes from gastric juices, the enzyme pepsin transforms proteins into amino acids, and lipase begins the metabolism of fats into fatty acids.

LARGE INTESTINE

The large intestine's functions are defecation and the reabsorption of water. The appendix is a small organ which has no function in the digestive process. ▶

COLON

CECUM

RECTUM

APPENDIX

The Circulation System, A Muscular Network

The body contains a network perfectly suited to carrying nutrients and energy to all the cells of the human body. Waste substances which are useless or harmful are transported to the organs equipped to expel them from the body.

The circulatory system carries out these two important functions: it disperses food and hormones, at the same time collecting waste products from the cells' metabolism, and it distributes oxygen throughout the whole body, while collecting the carbon dioxide which results from respiration.

Arteries, veins, and capillaries are the conductors along which the blood circulates—in an adult's body there are more than 60,000 miles of blood vessels. Arteries, which carry blood away from the heart, gradually become capillaries, tiny connecting ducts. These gradually transform themselves back into larger tubes called veins, which carry blood from

the separate organs back to the heart's chambers.

Because they must withstand the highest pressure, arteries have the strongest, most elastic walls. Veins have valves to prevent blood from flowing in the wrong direction. Thanks to the smooth musculature of the circulatory system's vessels, their diameter increases or decreases according to the physiological needs of each organ.

In the pulmonary circuit, blood full of carbon dioxide leaves the heart's right ventricle via the pulmonary artery and reaches the lungs, where it releases the carbon dioxide and absorbs oxygen. Then the pulmonary veins transport the oxygenated blood to the heart's left atrium.

▼

MINOR CIRCUIT

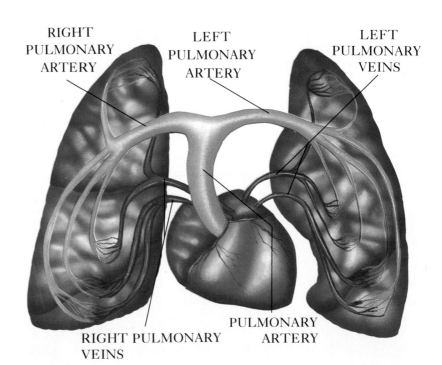

RIGHT PULMONARY ARTERY

LEFT PULMONARY ARTERY

LEFT PULMONARY VEINS

RIGHT PULMONARY VEINS

PULMONARY ARTERY

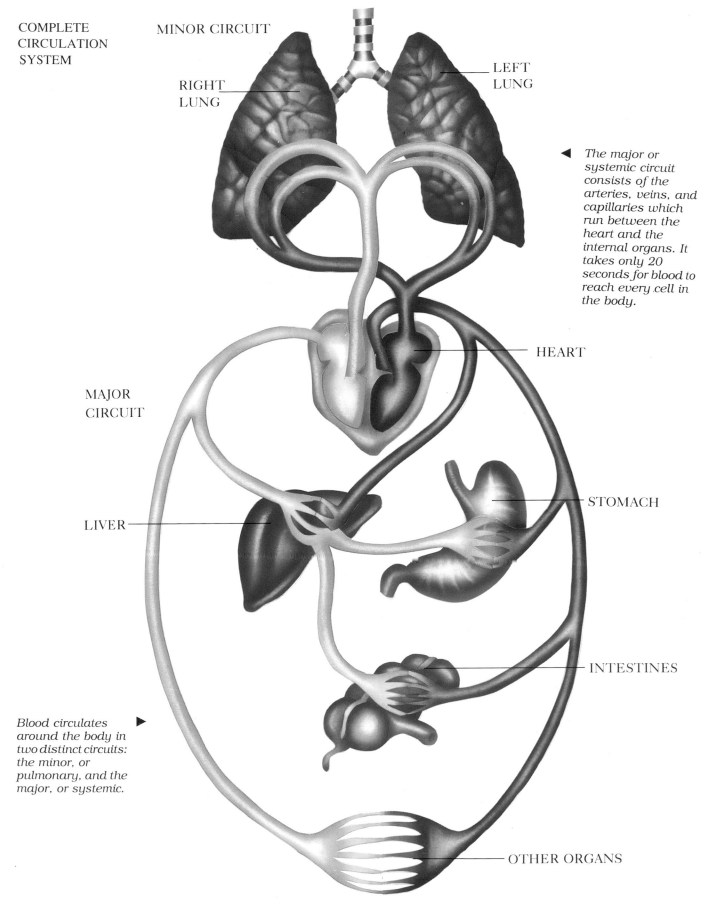

COMPLETE
CIRCULATION
SYSTEM

MINOR CIRCUIT

RIGHT
LUNG

LEFT
LUNG

◀ *The major or
systemic circuit
consists of the
arteries, veins, and
capillaries which
run between the
heart and the
internal organs. It
takes only 20
seconds for blood to
reach every cell in
the body.*

HEART

MAJOR
CIRCUIT

STOMACH

LIVER

INTESTINES

*Blood circulates
around the body in
two distinct circuits:
the minor, or
pulmonary, and the
major, or systemic.* ▶

OTHER ORGANS

The Most Important Muscle

For an organ no bigger than an adult's fist the heart has amazing power and durability. Nonstop through your whole life, the heart beats an average of 70 times per minute, pumping blood into the lungs with its right side and to the rest of the body with its left side.

The heart is constructed of a special kind of striated muscle, the myocardium or cardiac muscle, which is involuntary. These muscle cells are well-supplied with oxygen by a collection of coronary blood vessels. The heart's left side, which pumps blood through the entire body, is more muscular than the right side.

During a heartbeat the muscles contract, shortening and hardening the chambers of the heart. The contractions send blood from the heart's atria (upper chambers) through valves into the ventria (lower chambers) and then into the major blood vessels. This rhythmic contraction is the systolic pressure, which is followed by the diastolic pressure when the muscles relax and expand. Steady heartbeats create a wave of pressure forcing blood through the arteries which is referred to as a pulse.

Each side of the heart has two chambers. The upper one, the atrium, has small, thin walls and dilates when the blood enters. A valve leads into the lower chamber, the ventricle, which is larger with thick, muscular walls.

A view of the myocardium. These striated, involuntary fibers keep the heart pumping at a rate of nearly 100,000 beats per day. ▶

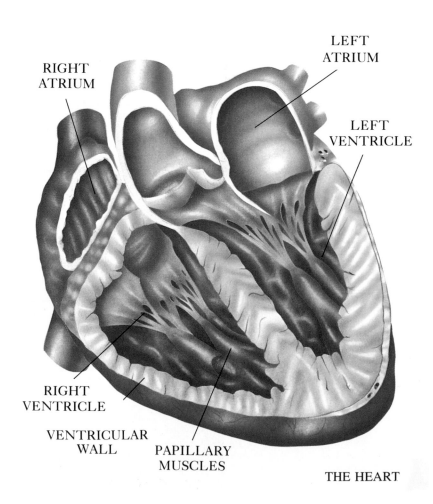

RIGHT ATRIUM

LEFT ATRIUM

LEFT VENTRICLE

RIGHT VENTRICLE

VENTRICULAR WALL

PAPILLARY MUSCLES

THE HEART

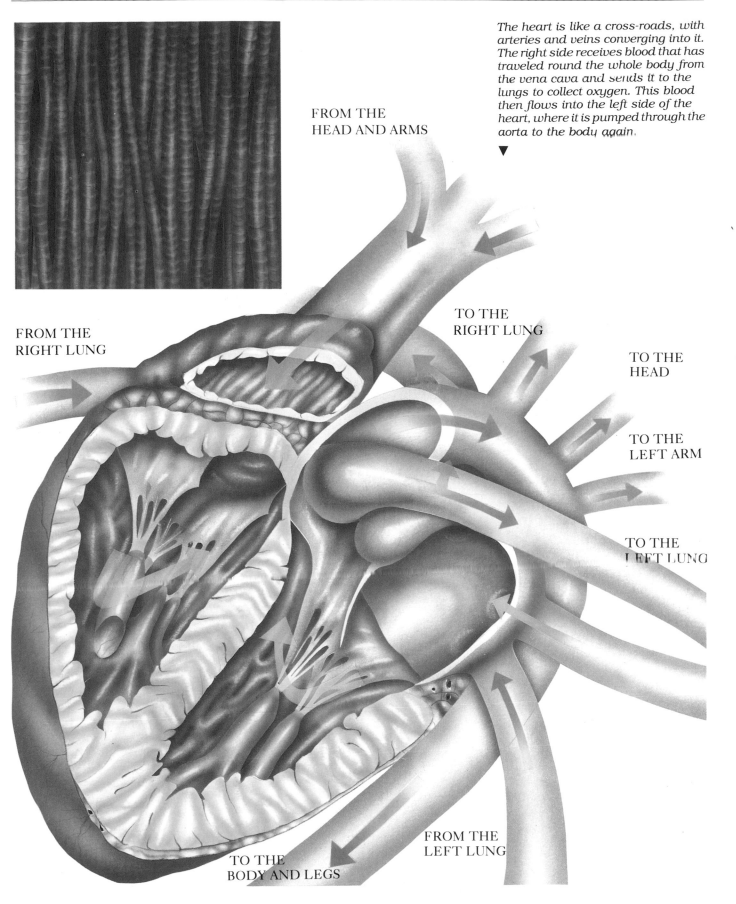

The heart is like a cross-roads, with arteries and veins converging into it. The right side receives blood that has traveled round the whole body from the vena cava and sends it to the lungs to collect oxygen. This blood then flows into the left side of the heart, where it is pumped through the aorta to the body again.
▼

FROM THE
HEAD AND ARMS

FROM THE
RIGHT LUNG

TO THE
RIGHT LUNG

TO THE
HEAD

TO THE
LEFT ARM

TO THE
LEFT LUNG

FROM THE
LEFT LUNG

TO THE
BODY AND LEGS

25

Muscles in Shape

Physical exercise is beneficial for keeping muscles fit and achieving a general level of good health. When you follow a regular, vigorous training program, muscle fibers form new actin and myosin filaments, forging bigger and stronger muscles. Exercises that require a few contractions of maximum force build strength, while numerous repetitions of lesser force enhance muscle tone.

Muscles require glucose, a carbohydrate found in foods like pasta, potatoes, and fruit, to make the energy which powers their work.

Eating a well-balanced diet should provide you with all the nutrients you need to sustain a healthy body.

Be aware of your capabilities, because overexertion can cause muscle stiffness, cramps, or injuries. Painful stiffness arises when an out-of-shape muscle is subjected to too much physical exercise, leaving a buildup of lactic acid. Train your muscles slowly and regularly to avoid stiffness. Cramps occur when a group of muscles are contracted suddenly. To prevent this, warm up the muscles before exercising and massage them gently.

Food provides the fuel we need to function, giving us energy and building the cells of the body. Vegetables, fresh fruit, grains, dairy products, fish, and meat contribute a range of nutrients, vitamins, and minerals to a healthy diet.

▼

IRON

CALCIUM

SODIUM

MAGNESIUM

POTASSIUM

FLUORIDE

IODINE

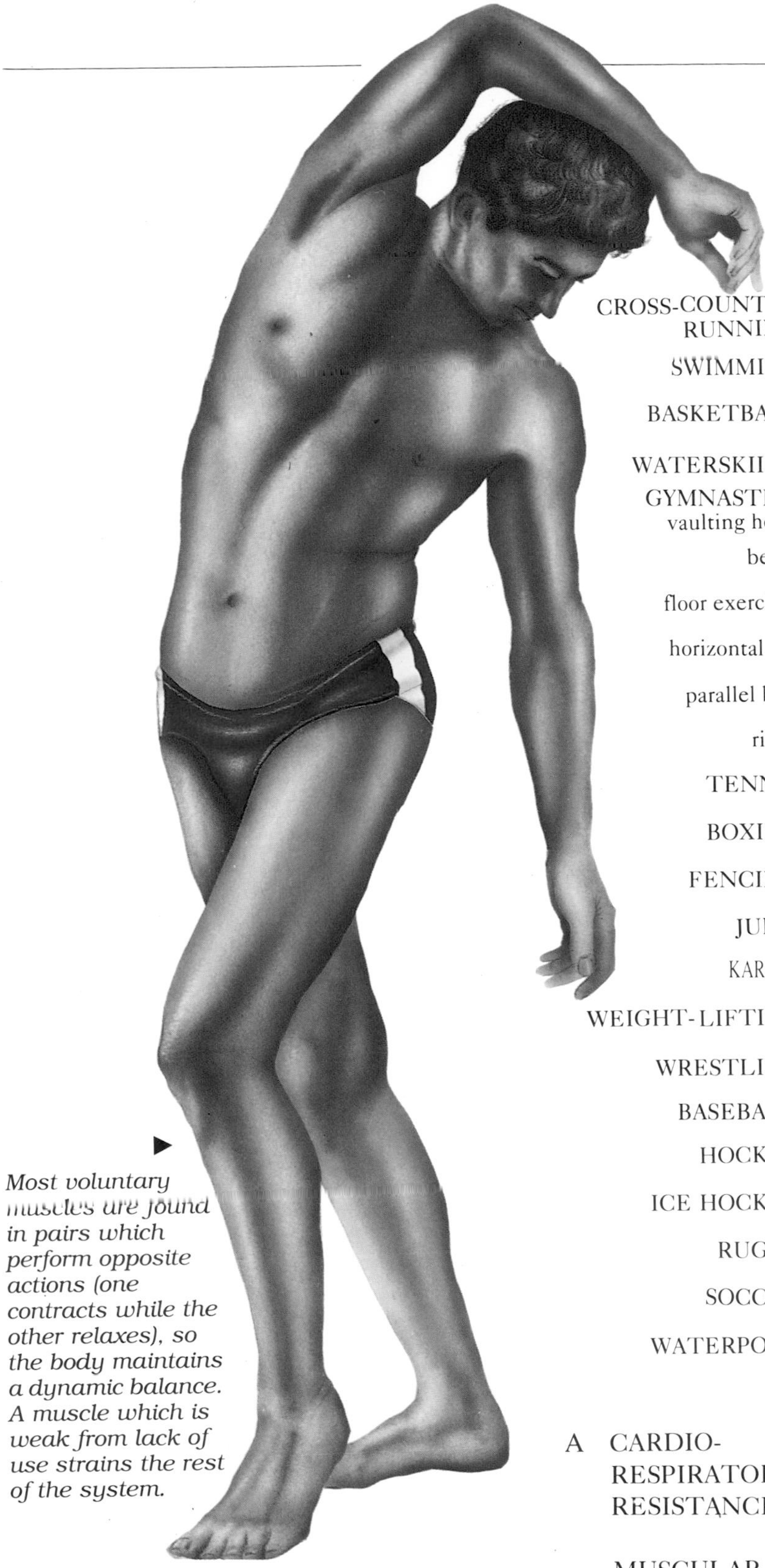

	BACK	SHOULDERS	ARMS	ABDOMEN	HIPS	LEGS	A
CROSS-COUNTRY RUNNING	●			●		● ●●	●
SWIMMING	●●	●	● ●●	●●	●	● ●●	●
BASKETBALL						● ●●	●
WATERSKIING	●		● ●	●		● ●	●
GYMNASTICS: vaulting horse	●		● ●●	●	●		
beam	●		●	●	●	● ●	
floor exercises	●	●	● ●●	●	●	●	
horizontal bar	●	●	● ●●	●			
parallel bars	●	●	● ●	●		●	
rings	●	●	● ●●		●		
TENNIS		●	●			● ●●	●
BOXING	●●		● ●●	●●		● ●●	●
FENCING			●		●	● ●	●
JUDO	●●		● ●●	●	●	● ●	●
KARATE	●●		● ●●	●	●	● ●●	●
WEIGHT-LIFTING	●●		● ●	●		● ●	
WRESTLING	●●	●	● ●●	●●	●	● ●	●
BASEBALL		●	●			●	
HOCKEY	●		●		●	● ●●	
ICE HOCKEY	●		●	●	●		●
RUGBY			●			● ●●	●
SOCCER						● ●●	●
WATERPOLO	●	●	● ●			●	●

▶

Most voluntary muscles are found in pairs which perform opposite actions (one contracts while the other relaxes), so the body maintains a dynamic balance. A muscle which is weak from lack of use strains the rest of the system.

A CARDIO-RESPIRATORY RESISTANCE

● MUSCULAR STRENGTH

● MUSCULAR RESISTANCE

● FLEXIBILITY

▲

Our bodies are designed for activity, with muscles that have the potential to be strong, agile, flexible, and precise. The table above charts which sports exercise which muscles.

Observing and Understanding

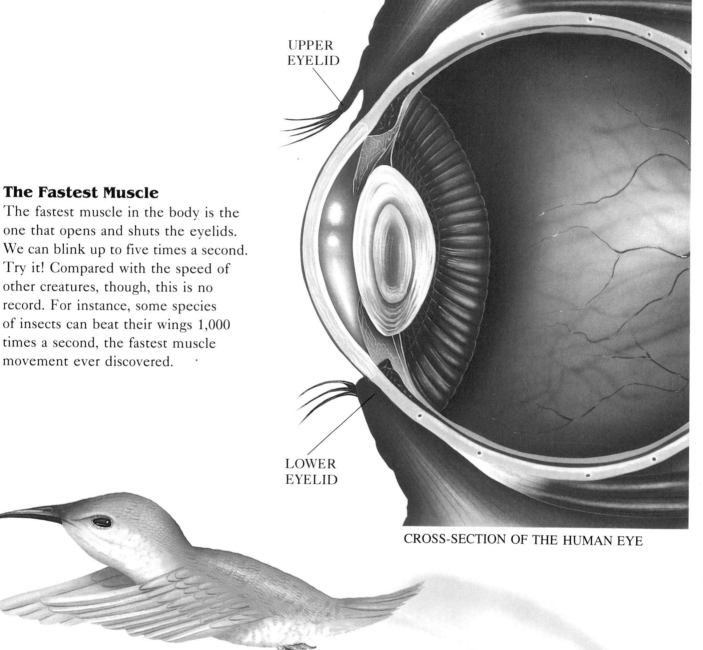

UPPER
EYELID

LOWER
EYELID

CROSS-SECTION OF THE HUMAN EYE

The Fastest Muscle

The fastest muscle in the body is the one that opens and shuts the eyelids. We can blink up to five times a second. Try it! Compared with the speed of other creatures, though, this is no record. For instance, some species of insects can beat their wings 1,000 times a second, the fastest muscle movement ever discovered.

▲
The hummingbird can stay still, suspended in mid-air while it sucks the nectar from a flower, thanks to its ability to beat its wings 55 times per second. It can also fly backwards when it has finished.

Muscular Mysteries

To experience a strange sensation, stand beneath a doorway and lift your arms until the backs of your hands touch the door jambs. Push with the backs of your hands and your wrists as hard as you can, counting slowly to thirty. Then step back and let your hands fall to your sides. What do you feel?

The brain, via the nerves, has been giving your muscles the order to raise your arms. When you suddenly step back from the doorway, some of the orders still haven't arrived at their destination, so the muscles take a couple of seconds to receive the last instructions.

Tremblers

The more you try to keep the muscles in your arms still, the more they tremble. Before beginning, gather the following materials: three paper clips, a knife, and a table. Stretch the paper clips into V-shaped wires and place them along the blade of the knife.

Stand next to a table and hold the knife in your right hand so that the tips of the wire just barely touch the table. Don't lean your arm on the table or steady the knife. Try and keep the knife and the wire still. Can you do it? What does the wire do?

What really happens? Inside the muscles there are always fibers that are contracted and fibers that are relaxed. In turn they alternate from one to the other. Each time they change, the muscle experiences a tiny shake, never permitting you to keep your arm absolutely still.

MATERIALS

A KNIFE

THREE PAPER CLIPS

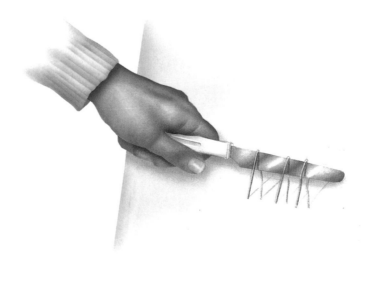

Glossary

artery *a large blood vessel that carries blood away from the heart*

atria *an upper chamber of the heart*

bolus *a ball of food that has been chewed and mixed with saliva*

capillary *a tiny connecting blood vessel*

cartilage *a tough tissue which often cushions the joints*

cellular respiration *the process by which muscle fibers turn glucose into fuel for energizing muscle contraction*

diaphragm *the muscle whose contractions allow the lungs to inhale and whose relaxations force the lungs to exhale*

fascicle *a small bundle of muscle fibers*

glucose *a sugar found in carbohydrates and fruits that provides energy to cells*

glycogen *the form of glucose stored in muscle*

joint *a movable link between two rigid parts of the body*

metabolism *the process by which a substance within a living organism is chemically broken down to release energy*

mitochondria *structures within muscle fibers that manufacture ATP, a source of energy for muscle contraction*

motor neuron *a nerve cell that transmits impulses for muscle contraction*

myocardium *the striated cardiac muscle found in the heart*

myofibril *a long, thin structure made of actin or myosin in a muscle fiber*

nucleus *a structure within a cell that is essential to cell functions such as reproduction and protein synthesis*

peristalsis *the contractions of smooth muscles which push food through the digestive tract*

pulse *the regular wave of pressure through the arteries, caused by the beating of the heart*

sarcolemma *the membrane surrounding a skeletal muscle fiber*

skeletal muscle *a striated muscle attached to bone that is responsible for voluntary movements*

smooth muscle *a muscle responsible for automatic actions*

tendon *connective tissue attaching muscle to bone*

vein *a large blood vessel that delivers blood to the heart*

ventria *a lower chamber of the heart*

Index